AMERICAN HEROES

JOHN LEWIS
CIVIL RIGHTS LEADER

by Katie Chanez

Pogo Books, an imprint of Jump! Library by FlutterBee

Ideas for Parents and Teachers

Pogo Books let children practice reading informational text while introducing them to nonfiction features such as headings, labels, sidebars, maps, and diagrams, as well as a table of contents, glossary, and index.

Carefully leveled text with a strong photo match offers early fluent readers the support they need to succeed.

Before Reading

- "Walk" through the book and point out the various nonfiction features. Ask the student what purpose each feature serves.
- Look at the glossary together. Read and discuss the words.

During Reading

- Have the child read the book independently.
- Invite them to list questions that arise from reading.

After Reading

- Discuss the child's questions. Talk about how they might find answers to those questions.
- Prompt the child to think more. Ask: Have you ever stood up for something you thought was right? What was that like?

Pogo Books are published by Jump!
3500 American Blvd W, Suite 150
Bloomington, MN 55431
www.jumplibrary.com

Jump! is a division of FlutterBee Education Group.

Library of Congress Cataloging-in-Publication Data is available at www.loc.gov or upon request from the publisher.

ISBN: 979-8-89662-361-8 (hardcover)
ISBN: 979-8-89662-362-5 (paperback)
ISBN: 979-8-89662-363-2 (ebook)

Editor: Alyssa Sorenson
Designer: Molly Ballanger

Photo Credits: Olivier Douliery/Sipa USA/AP Images, cover; Kathy Hutchins/Shutterstock, 1; The New York Public Library, 3; Chip Somodevilla/Getty, 4; Library of Congress, 5, 10-11; Bettmann/Getty, 6-7, 8, 9, 10; Tracy Sugarman/Jackson State University/Getty, 12-13; Alpha Historica/Alamy, 14-15; Smith Archive/Alamy, 16-17; Laura Patterson/CQ Roll Call/Getty, 18; Pamela Au/Shutterstock, 19; Carolyn Kaster/AP Images, 20-21; Bill Clark/CQ Roll Call/Getty, 23.

Printed in the United States of America at Corporate Graphics in North Mankato, Minnesota.

TABLE OF CONTENTS

CHAPTER 1

EARLY LIFE

John Lewis worked in **Congress**. He fought for people's **rights**.

John was born on February 21, 1940. He lived in Alabama. Many southern U.S. states were **segregated** then. Black people could not drink from the same drinking fountains as white people. They could not go to the same places. Places for Black people were often not nice.

sit-in

John found this unfair. He joined the **Civil Rights** Movement. When he was 20, he joined sit-ins in Nashville, Tennessee. Black **college** students went to a whites-only restaurant. It would not give them food. They did homework instead. White cops arrested them. This upset some people. They spoke out. Nashville got rid of segregation!

CHAPTER 2

"GOOD TROUBLE"

John kept getting into what he called "good trouble." In 1961, he joined the Freedom Rides. The **U.S. Supreme Court** said buses that traveled between states could not be segregated. Freedom Riders rode these buses to test this.

This made white people angry. John and other riders were arrested many times. But others saw what they were doing. They took their own Freedom Rides. Later that year, segregation at bus stations ended.

In 1963, John joined other civil rights leaders. They had a large **protest** in Washington, D.C. It became known as the March on Washington. John gave a speech. He spoke out about violence against Black people.

DID YOU KNOW?

More than 250,000 people came to the protest. Radio and television stations were there, too. They shared it with the rest of the country.

WE DEMAND AN FEPC LAW NOW!
UAW SAYS JOBS and FREEDOM FOR Every American
FIRST CLASS CITIZENS CAN VOTE D.C. WANTS HOME RULE
WE DEMAND AN END TO BIAS NOW!
WE MARCH FOR JOBS FOR ALL A DECENT PAY NOW!
Washington Board of Rabbis

Many Black people in Mississippi were kept from voting. They had to pass tests to **register** to vote. Those who didn't pass didn't get a say in picking their leaders. In 1964, John helped. How? He helped bring teachers to Mississippi. They helped Black people practice reading and writing for the test. They learned how to pass.

WHAT DO YOU THINK?

Some states used tests to stop people from voting. They made people prove they could read and write English. Do you think this was fair? Why or why not?

80 TH
THIS LA
LEFT TURN
LANE
EDMUND PETTUS BRIDGE

In February 1965, police officers attacked protestors in Selma, Alabama. A Black man was killed. **Activists** decided to hold a march. They would walk from Selma to Montgomery, Alabama. Montgomery is the state capital. John led the march across a Selma bridge.

Police were waiting. They told the marchers to leave. They did not. The police threw **tear gas**. Some beat marchers. John was badly hurt. Americans saw it on the news. They became angry. They called for change. Later that year, President Lyndon B. Johnson signed the Voting Rights Act. This gave everyone an equal chance to vote.

TAKE A LOOK!

Marchers started in Selma. They were supposed to go to Montgomery. They were stopped at the bridge. Take a look.

CHAPTER 3

JOINING POLITICS

John wanted to help more people. He ran for Congress. He was **elected** in 1986. As part of Congress, John fought for equal rights for everyone.

In 1988, John wanted to create a Black history museum. Congress said no. He kept bringing it up. Congress finally agreed in 2003. The National Museum of African American History and Culture opened in Washington, D.C. in 2016.

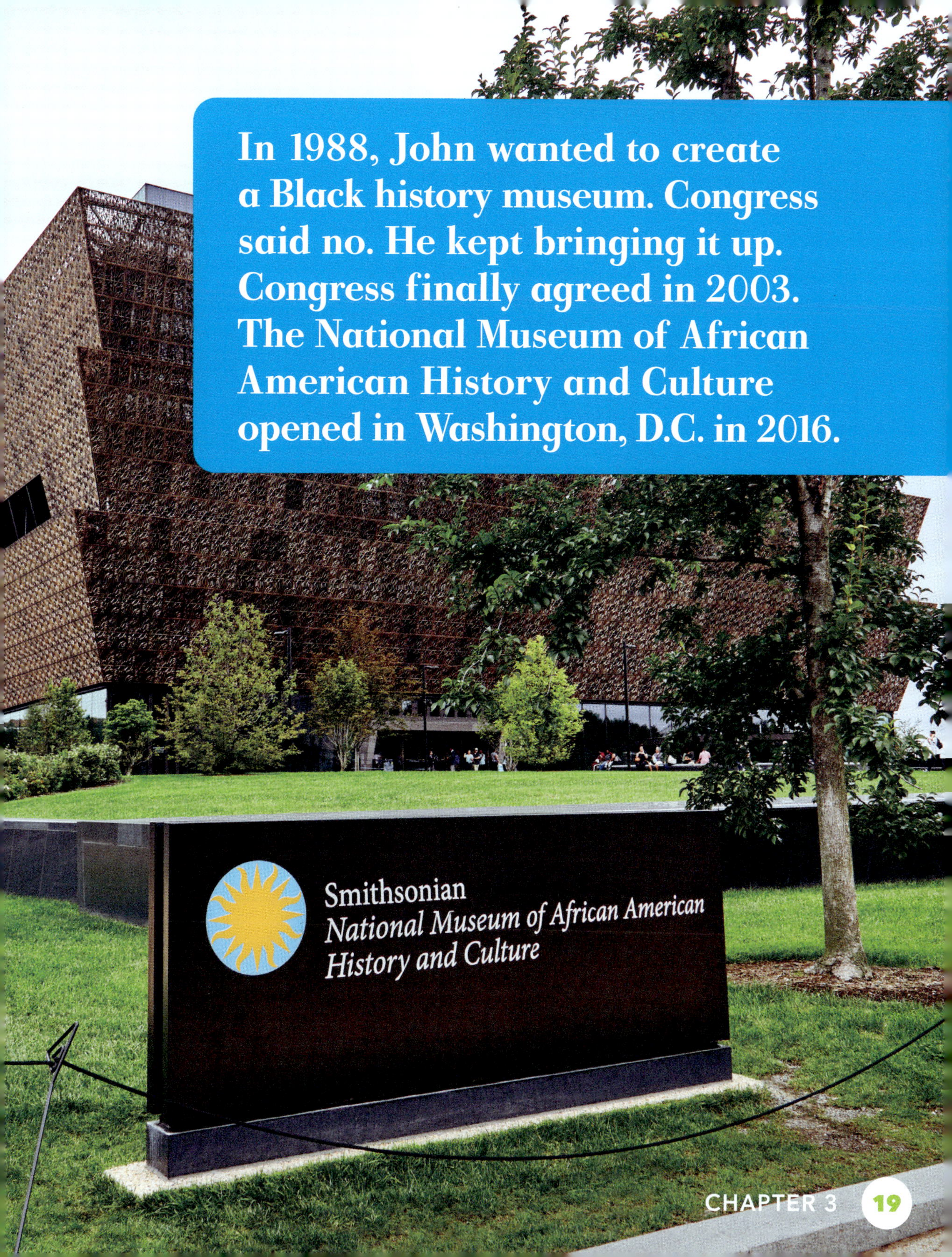

Presidential Medal of Freedom

In 2011, President Barack Obama gave John the Presidential Medal of Freedom. This is an award. It is given to people who make the United States better.

John died on July 17, 2020. People remember him. His work still **inspires** others to fight for equality.

WHAT DO YOU THINK?

It can be hard to stand up for others. John was often hurt or arrested. Why do you think he kept trying?

QUICK FACTS & TOOLS

TIMELINE

What are big events in John Lewis' life? Take a look!

FEBRUARY 21, 1940
John Robert Lewis is born near Troy, Alabama.

1957
John moves to Nashville, Tennessee, to go to college. He becomes a Baptist minister.

1960
John and other students do a sit-in at a whites-only restaurant in Nashville.

1961
John spends the summer doing Freedom Rides. He is attacked and arrested many times.

AUGUST 28, 1963
John speaks to thousands of people during the March on Washington.

MARCH 7, 1965
John leads a march from Selma to Montgomery, Alabama. He and other marchers are attacked. The day becomes known as Bloody Sunday.

1986-2020
John serves in Congress.

2011
John receives the Presidential Medal of Freedom.

JULY 17, 2020
John dies at age 80. People remember and honor his fight for equality.

GLOSSARY

activists: People who support a cause and believe in taking action to change things.

civil rights: Things citizens are guaranteed and able to do.

college: A place that teaches higher learning beyond high school.

Congress: The part of the U.S. government that makes laws.

elected: Chosen by people who vote.

inspires: Influences or encourages someone to do something.

protest: To demonstrate or make statements against something.

register: To be added to an official list.

rights: Things you are allowed to do.

segregated: Separated or kept apart from the main group.

tear gas: A gas that irritates the eyes, throat, lungs, and skin and is used by law enforcement to break up crowds.

U.S. Supreme Court: The highest U.S. court that upholds the U.S. Constitution and laws.

INDEX

TO LEARN MORE

Finding more information is as easy as 1, 2, 3.

1. Go to www.factsurfer.com
2. Enter "John Lewis" into the search box.
3. Choose your book to see a list of websites.

FACT SURFER